# "Hello Birdie!"

## Tale of a Classroom Pet
## Based on a true story

BY DENISE ABDA NAHAL

*Denise Abda Nahal*

Order this book online at www.trafford.com
or email orders@trafford.com

Most Trafford titles are also available at major online book retailers.

Printed in the United States of America.

ISBN: 978-1-4669-6822-6 (sc)
978-1-4669-6821-9 (e)


Trafford rev. 11/20/2012

 www.trafford.com

North America & international
toll-free: 1 888 232 4444 (USA & Canada)
phone: 250 383 6864 • fax: 812 355 4082

Dedication:

For "Bird lovers" everywhere. -D.A.N.

With Special thanks to:
Henry, Dennis and Henry James for all their love and support.

1

"Hello Birdie!" chirped the brightly colored Amazon parrot. "Hello Birdie!" Rubric the parrot was pacing across the top of his cage like a tight rope walker. "Hello Birdie!" he called out once again. Rubric was excited; it was the first day of school and his first day as classroom pet!

The friendly parrot knew being a classroom pet was very important but he had never even been in a school before. He didn't know what to expect!

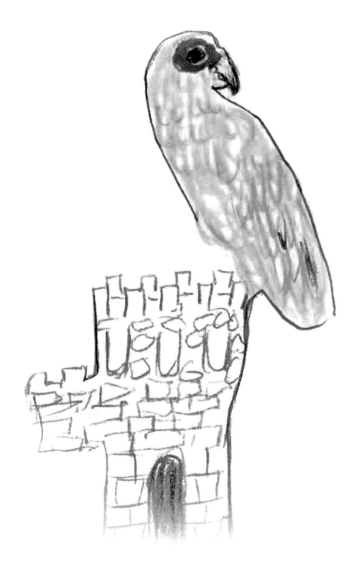

The pretty green bird may have been the smallest of Amazon parrots,
but he had a great big heart and he wanted to do his best.

The day he joined our first grade classroom, Rubric was ready for anything. Rubric was a natural!  When the school bell rang, on that first day of a new school year, he hopped to the top of his climbing tree and rang his own little toy bell!

Rubric greeted the students with his friendly "Hello Birdie!" and a few silly "gymnastics" on his tree. Twisting, turning and flipping from branch to branch, he delighted every student he met.

Rubric chimed in during the Pledge of Allegiance and "sang" right along to our patriotic song with his cheery squawks and tweets. With a little encouragement he settled right down when the children began their work.

Rubric would always squawk loudly if anyone was misbehaving. When he heard a student teasing or saying unkind words he'd call out his friendly greeting, "Hello Birdie, Pretty Birdie, Pretty Rubric". It seemed he was reminding the students that kind words were much better than mean words. Soon the children would laugh and a friendship instead of a quarrel would begin.

The students were always happy to share a blueberry, strawberry
or pretzel with the happy little bird. Rubric's berry coated beak was
a sure sign of his appreciation! The children quickly realized how
important and rewarding it was to care and to share. "Good Birdie!"
he'd chatter.

Rubric loved the children and he loved school. He brought his best to school every single day, making our classroom a special place indeed.

In his own quirky way Rubric taught the children how to make friends
and how to be a good friend. Rubric was always cheerful, friendly and
fun loving.

The children, Rubric greeted each and every day, learned important lessons from the clever Amazon parrot.  You can too!

Remember:

Always start each day with a friendly happy greeting.  "Hello Birdie!"

Use kind words; they are much better than hurtful words.  "Pretty Birdie!"

Do your best every day. Be a caring and sharing friend.  "Good Birdie, Good Birdie!"

Rubric is a White-fronted Amazon Parrot. For over 15 years Rubric touched the lives of hundreds of students and their families at Bell Top Elementary School in Troy, New York. Rubric lives with his owner, retired teacher, Denise Abda Nahal in East Greenbush, New York.